Communication:
What Does It Mean to Me?

A "Contract for Communication" that will promote understanding between individuals with autism or Asperger's and their families, teachers, therapists, co-workers, and many more!

Catherine Faherty

Communication: What Does It Mean to Me?

All marketing and publishing rights guaranteed to and reserved by

FUTURE HORIZONS INC.

721 W. Abram Street
Arlington, Texas 76013
800-489-0727
817-277-0727
817-277-2270 (fax)
E-mail: info@FHautism.com
www.FHautism.com

Publisher's Cataloging-In-Publication Data
(Prepared by The Donohue Group, Inc.)

Faherty, Catherine.

   Communication : what does it mean to me? / Catherine Faherty.

   p. ; cm.

"A 'Contract for Communication' that will promote understanding between individuals with autism or Asperger's and their families, teachers, therapists, co-workers, and many more!"
   Includes bibliographical references and index.
   ISBN: 978-1-935274-17-9

   1. Autistic children--Means of communication. 2. Asperger's syndrome--Patients--Care. 3. Communicative disorders in children--Treatment--Popular works. 4. Autism spectrum disorders--Treatment--Popular works. I. Title.

RJ506.A9 F34 2010
618.928/588/2

Do not say a little in many words,
but a great deal in a few.

—Pythagoras

*To all my communication partners on the spectrum,
especially the members of the Social Group, past and present,
for teaching me what helps—and what doesn't help.*

*With special appreciation for Carolyn Ogburn and Jon
Blalock, my colleagues at the Asheville TEACCH Center,
whose creative use of Communication Forms and other
written communication strategies is inspiring.*

TABLE OF CONTENTS

INTRODUCTION

What is the Contract for Communication?

The Contract for Communication distills a few simple rules to improve communication and presents them as a unique user-friendly resource. It consists of guidelines, described as "agreements" to be made between communication partners.

It is no surprise that plenty of communication problems can occur between people with ASD and their neurotypical communication partners; after all, there is much variation among people, and there are endless individual issues that can interfere with harmonious interaction. Not all misunderstanding will be eliminated by the agreements proposed in the Contract for Communication. However, by following these straightforward guidelines, the chances of miscommunication and misunderstanding—on both sides—may greatly decrease. It is a place to start. My hope is that mutual understanding and authentic communication will flourish.

About the Agreements

The Contract for Communication includes five agreements for each communication partner. The first set of agreements (Part 1) is meant for the neurotypical communication partner and the second set of agreements (Part 2) is meant for the communication partner with ASD. Each of these two groups of communicators has its own general characteristics, assumptions, and quirks; which is why I have proposed a unique set of agreements for each group.

Miscommunication and misunderstanding can result from a mismatched style of communicating. In order to reach through these differences and meet "the other" in a place of clarity, ease, and understanding, each communication partner must adapt or modify at least some parts of his or her automatic way of communicating. I propose to those who sincerely desire to better understand and relate to their communication partner, that they adopt the agreements in this Contract for Communication.

Miscommunication and misunderstanding can result from a mismatched style of communicating.

The beauty of the Contract for Communication is that both sets of agreements can be described as "win-win." Both communication partners benefit from every agreement.

Refer to the Glossary

Please refer to the Glossary for explanations of the following terms used in this Contract for Communication. They are listed in alphabetical order.

- Agreement
- ASD
- Aspie
- Autism-friendlly
- Autism spectrum disorder
- Communication
- Communication partner
- Communication style
- Considerate
- Contract
- Courteous
- Miscommunication
- Misunderstanding
- Neurotypical
- NT
- On the spectrum
- Self-advocacy
- Win-win

A Confession about Terminology

Although I am grateful for my talent in communicating with the written word, I am often frustrated by a lack of ability to say exactly what I know or feel to be true and accurate.

This is most apparent when I use the following words to describe children and adults: *on the autism spectrum, on the spectrum, neurotypical, ASD,* and *NT*; and the use of the preposition *with* [ASD or Asperger's]. Of course the essence of each person cannot be labeled or described by these terms. My intent in using these terms is to communicate clearly and effectively to the reader, with the hope that this document will benefit its earnest users.

> We should acknowledge differences, we should greet differences, until difference makes no difference anymore.

At the same time, I acknowledge and respect those people with ASD who wholeheartedly embrace the terms *autistic, autie, Asperger's,* or *Aspie* as a personal identification.

It is in this spirit that I repeat here the opening quote of my book *Asperger's … What Does It Mean to Me? A Workbook Explaining Self-awareness and Life Lessons to the Child or Youth with High-functioning Autism or Asperger's.* It reads:

> *We should acknowledge differences, we should greet differences,*
> *until difference makes no difference anymore.*
> —Adela A. Allen

Special Note for Parents and Teachers of Young Children

If you are a neurotypical family member or teacher of young children with ASD, or a communication partner of those who are not able to read or understand Part 2: The ASD Agreements, your relationship may still benefit by *your* adhering to the applicable agreements in Part 1: The NT Agreements. Moreover, your familiarity with the agreements recommended for individuals with ASD (Part 2) may trigger ideas for vital and fundamental goals to work toward as your child grows.

Author's Point of View

For the past twenty-five years, I have interacted with people on the spectrum, young and old, first as an elementary school teacher, and then as a psychoeducational therapist, colleague, and friend. It became clear to me in 1985 while teaching in a model TEACCH classroom in Asheville, North Carolina, that although we neurotypical teachers and parents can quickly identify the need for behavioral change in the child with ASD, *a change in behavior—and attitude—must simultaneously occur within us.* Working with children, teens, and adults on the spectrum, I am learning to listen—really listen—to find out what it is *they* need and what it is *they* yearn for. What are *their* assumptions and concerns? What would *they ask me,* if they would, or could? Of course getting this information may not always be easy.

> Although teachers and families are quick to see a need for change in the person with ASD, they must also make changes in their own behavior.

The ideas I present in the Contract for Communication represent a few of the most essential practices I have learned, discovered through trial and error, used extensively, modeled in my books, and taught in workshops, to improve authentic communication. The fact that there are *two* sets of agreements (one for NT communicators and one for ASD communicators) ensure that the necessary work to improve communication is shared. In TEACCH, our passion and our work emerge from a foundation of acceptance and respect, which you will no doubt experience as you read the Contract for Communication.

For more information about the author's background and current work, see the biographical information in the About the Author section, page 107.

Complementary User-Friendly Information

I refer the reader to the following complementary user-friendly chapters directly related to this Contract for Communication in my previous interactive books, below:

In the book, *Asperger's: What Does It Mean to Me? A Workbook Explaining Self-Awareness and Life Lessons to Youth and Children with High Functioning Autism or Asperger's,* see Chapter 6 (Understanding), Chapter 7 (Thoughts), and Chapter 8 (Communication).

In the book, *Understanding Death and Illness and What They Teach About Life: An Interactive Guide for Individuals with Autism or Asperger's and Their Loved Ones,* see Chapter 5 (Communication) and Chapter 16 (What People May Learn About Life When Facing Death), which covers positive aspects of living a good life.

The NT Agreements

In this section, five agreements are suggested to neurotypical family members, teachers, students, therapists, employers, employees, co-workers, clients, neighbors, and friends of children and adults with ASD, who desire to improve their mutual communication.

~

The notion of implied meaning is the root of misunderstanding.

—Eric Parslow

About the NT Agreements

It will take practice—as most worthwhile endeavors do—but if you try your best to keep your agreements and honor this Contract for Communication, you will more likely succeed in strengthening your understanding of the important person or people with ASD in your life, while building a more courteous, harmonious, and mutually rewarding connection.

Every child and adult, ASD and NT, has a unique and distinctive way of communicating. Depending on our day-to-day circumstances, the way we express ourselves—and our ability to understand others—will vary. For these reasons, you will find that one or more of the NT Agreements may make a positive impact on communication between you and the person you know with ASD.

> You will need to modify your natural and automatic way of interacting as you strive to become an autism-friendly communicator.

In this section, you will find five suggested agreements for neurotypical communication partners of verbal children and adults with ASD or Asperger's. Following each agreement is my rationale for its inclusion in the Contract for Communication.

These five NT agreements make up Part 1 of the Contract for Communication.

The official document, for your signature, is located on pages 17-18.

NT Agreement #1

Wait. Don't expect (or insist on) immediate verbal responses from your communication partner with ASD.

Why keep this agreement?

Auditory processing is often complicated by ASD. Many children and adults on the spectrum struggle at some time or another with incomplete understanding when the information they are given is purely verbal. Even for those whose speech is highly developed, listening comprehension skills are often compromised. For many, it takes time to process what they are hearing, making it difficult to respond in the moment, as typically expected. If your communication partner on the spectrum avoids conversations, or if one or both of you become frustrated when trying to communicate, this could be one of the reasons why.

> Even for those whose speech is highly developed, listening comprehension skills are often compromised.

An added obstacle to your ASD communication partner's ability to process and respond to you during conversation is his or her anxiety level. Many people with Asperger's explain that their heightened anxiety dramatically affects their ability to comprehend spoken language—as well as their ability to truly express themselves through speech. It is compounded by the well-documented fact that children and adults with ASD function daily with a higher level of anxiety than most of their neurotypical peers.

Your communication partner's lack of response, or delayed response, during conversation can lead to confusion and misunderstanding on your part. You may mistakenly conclude that his or her silence means that you are being ignored, or that he or she must be uncooperative, stubborn, or angry, and therefore rudely refusing to interact with you. The possibilities for misunderstanding abound.

Or, your communication partner may habitually respond with the same phrase, time after time. Many children and adults with ASD have learned that they are supposed to answer when spoken to, resulting in their automatic response—which may not really reflect their true thoughts or feelings. Typical routine responses are phrases such as: "I don't know," "Okay," "I'm not sure," "You betcha," "If you insist," or _____ (yours to fill in.)

One of the most distressing consequences from expecting or insisting on an immediate verbal response from your communication partner with ASD is that you run the risk of forcing him or her to say something—anything—to complete the interaction. In a sense you are teaching your child (or student, friend, client, co-worker, etc.) that it is more important to say something that sounds plausible—but is meaningless—than to really think about the topic, identify his or her own truth, and subsequently express it to others.

By waiting patiently for a response without pressuring your communication partner with ASD, you will change your role in the non-communicative routine. Give your communication partner more time—more time than you think is needed. Don't repeat or re-phrase the question. Allow the quiet in which he or she can more easily process the information and find his or her own words that accurately reflect what is true. If you find it difficult to wait without talking, try counting silently to yourself. This will give you something to do while you wait!

> Be quiet. Give him time to process the information and find the words which accurately reflect what is true.

Zosia Zaks, in her book, *Positive Strategies for Autistic Adults*, writes that she and her partner have come up with something that works for them when they are in discussion. Zosia holds up a card on which is written "Processing," reminding her communication partner that she is not being ignored, thus allowing Zosia more time to think. You may want to follow Zosia's example and consider using a "Processing" sign, or agree on another signal when more time is needed by your communication partner with ASD.

If your communication partner on the spectrum is feeling anxious or overwhelmed, or slipping into a routine, meaningless response, you could suggest a future time when the discussion could be continued. Add it to the day's checklist of events, the daily schedule; or write on the weekly calendar when the topic can be continued. You may also try using a *written strategy* as an alternative or an adjunct to talking. Ideas for written strategies are suggested later in NT Agreements #3 and #4.

NT Agreement #2

Speak literally and concretely. Avoid hinting and indirectness. Say what you mean, and mean what you say. Less "chat" is better.

Why keep this agreement?

It is well-documented that children and adults with ASD or Asperger's rely on precision, accuracy, and clarity of language which is free of ambiguity, implied, or hidden meaning. Anything other than that may create confusion and misunderstanding, while heightening anxiety. It is autism-friendly—respectful and considerate to those with ASD—to communicate in a literal and concrete manner, even though many neurotypical communicators may consider such a direct manner too blunt or impolite.

> It is respectful to communicate literally, even though many NT communicators consider such a direct manner impolite or unnecessary.

When you are feeling nervous, insecure, or uncomfortable talking about a topic, you probably run the risk of "beating around the bush," being unintentionally obscure, or otherwise communicating indirectly. At these times, be vigilant! The very moment you are introducing a "difficult issue" or a topic that feels awkward to discuss, is the moment to remind yourself of this second NT Agreement.

Children and adults on the autism spectrum have taught me that it is imperative to communicate most clearly about things that are the most difficult to understand. For examples of communicating clearly about "difficult" subjects, see Appendix C, the section containing book excerpts from *Understanding Death and Illness and What They Teach About Life: An Interactive Guide for Individuals with Autism or Asperger's and their Loved Ones.*

So, speak (or write) clearly and to the point, calmly saying **exactly** what you wish to communicate. By keeping this agreement, you will be assured that what your communication partner heard is more likely to match what you intended to say.

It truly is a respectful and autism-friendly way to communicate; and often appreciated by those not on the autism spectrum, too!

NT Agreement #3

Provide information. Do not assume that the person "knows" what you think "everyone knows."

Why keep this agreement?

From the point of view of a person on the spectrum, there are countless situations, events, and circumstances that simply make no sense. The underlying rationale of a great number of the most well-respected strategies recommended to teachers and parents of children with ASD is to clarify, define, and provide information. Most adults with ASD, as well, greatly appreciate being filled in as to the reasons and explanations for what is happening at home, in relationships, and at work, especially if the event involves common assumptions based on widespread typical social perceptions.

> Provide relevant details and critical background facts about the topic of discussion, so your communication partner can make the pertinent connections, reflecting and identifying his or her own truths.

From your communication partner's point of view, strive to be a safe person from whom he or she is assured of getting clear answers and receiving direct information. Listen when questions are asked of you, and try not to read too much into the question. Answer the question that is being asked—not what you imagine he or she is asking. You can then follow up with specific questions verbally or in written form, if you suspect he or she may have unspoken questions.

Together with your communication partner, refer to dictionaries, encyclopedias, and reference websites that supply definitions, facts, and general information on specific topics. By looking up definitions together and researching information about the current topic of conversation, both communication partners will be assured that they are really talking about the same thing.

> This practice helps to build a foundation for self-knowledge, and in turn, makes authentic communication possible.

Examples of well-respected, autism-friendly practices are found in TEACCH Structured Teaching, pioneered and taught by the TEACCH Program (teacch.com) and Social Stories™ as taught by The Gray Center for Social Learning and Understanding (thegraycenter.org). Below are summaries of the type of information provided by TEACCH strategies Social Stories™.

Physical Organization. Clarifies "where" specific things take place. Offers concrete information about where to sit, stand, work, engage in activities, and otherwise organize the environment. Physical structure helps modulate sensory stimulation such as sights, sounds, and a busy environment; and organizes necessary materials and items.

Schedule and/or Checklist for the Day. Clarifies "when" specific events or activities are to take place. Helps the person predict upcoming changes and variations from day to day, and to see the big picture of the day. Teaches flexibility.

Work Systems. Clarifies in a visual manner these four questions about a series of assignments or activities: What am I supposed to do?   How many things am I supposed to do? How do I know when I'm finished? and What comes next?

Structured Social Activities. Clarifies all of the above in social situations (which typically offer very little structure or information in autism-friendly ways.) Use schedules and work systems in social activities. Design activities based on the assessment of your communication partner's level of Social Comfort as taught by TEACCH.

Visual Cues. Offers visual prompts in situations that require self-initiation and and/or pragmatic communication skills.

Social Stories™ . Social Stories™ describe a situation, skill, or concept, explaining relevant social cues, perspectives, and common responses in a specifically defined style. The writing process inherently involves discovering the individual perspective of the person on the spectrum, while learning more about one's hidden expectations. Information is provided in a reassuring manner, often leading to greater understanding.

Whenever possible, be trained in the use of these strategies properly and appropriately. Always consider the point of view of your communication partner when using any strategy. *One size does NOT fit all!*

NT Agreement #4

Help your communication partner's self-expression. Provide tools: paper, pen, computer keyboard, and/or Communication Forms to facilitate authentic communication.

Why keep this agreement?

Often it is just plain easier for your communication partner on the spectrum to identify what he or she honestly thinks or feels with the support of *visual methods to aid communication.* This is true for adolescents and adults, as well as for children. Experiment with pen, paper, and computer keyboard to see if and when these communication tools allow greater ease, encourage earnest self-awareness, and help to assure genuine communication.

Communication Forms are typically multiple-choice and/or fill-in-the-blank lists to engage the communicator and support self-knowledge by inviting him or her to discover and then indicate what is personally true. I titled them "Communication Forms" because after filling them out, the word "communication" serves as a reminder to share the information with someone. These forms help the communicator on the spectrum connect with others by making it easy to share his or her personal thoughts and structure further interaction.

> Communication Forms engage the communicator and support self-knowledge by making it easier to identify and indicate what is personally true.

Helpful hints about creating your own Communication Forms, along with a variety of examples can be found in the Appendices at the end of this book. Hundreds of examples of Communication Forms can be found in other books by this author.

Types of communication tools, strategies, and Communication Forms are described on these two pages. More information and examples can be found in the Appendices.

Communication Forms with Checklists

Like a "multiple choice test," this type of Communication Form helps to eliminate extraneous and/or irrelevant information that may interfere with his or her ability to focus on the topic at hand. Reading possible options and checking an empty box, circling, or highlighting a phrase or sentence may allow the person on the spectrum to more easily reflect on the relevant issues and identify honest personal responses. These communication forms often begin with the instruction, *"I will check (or mark) what is true for me."* For those who have trouble retrieving or finding the words to identify what is true for them, seeing a list of possible options may help eliminate what is NOT true and identify what IS true.

Communication Forms with Fill-in-the-Blanks

Often, Communication Forms with checklists include options to write on blank lines within a particular entry on the list, or as a blank line at the end of the list.

Blank Catagorizing Lists

Another type of Communication Form may be structured by dividing the page into lists of blanks or empty frames underneath headings which label the relevant categories. The child or adult fills in the blanks underneath each category with facts; or with his or her thoughts, ideas, feelings, and/or information which is true for him or her. People may find a greater ease in expressing their thoughts in this way since it allows them to sort information into categories, therefore organizing their thinking and ideas in a precise, orderly, rational, and linear fashion.

Using this format as part of the act of communicating is well-suited for many children and adults on the spectrum.

Computer Conversations

Even before email became a part of life, I discovered that sitting side by side with my communication partner with ASD at the computer keyboard made it easier, and in some cases, possible for the first time to have a real conversation. Giving information, asking questions, and responding in a written manner (while talking, *or instead of talking*) is a straightforward method which clearly structures the mechanics— whose turn it is to listen (read) and whose turn it is to talk (type). A quiet environment in which to recieve information visually without talking, helps many people with ASD process and respond with less anxiety and greater ease. There is automatically less auditory stimulation and less expectation to respond verbally. Another advantage of a Computer Conversation is that when finished, it can be printed and carried away by your communication partner to re-read later.

Chatting on the Internet could be considered a high-tech and long-distance version of Computer Conversations.

Emails and Letters

Helpful for the same reasons as Computer Conversations, these methods additionally eliminate pressure to respond in the moment.

Pen and Paper

There are times when a quiet conversation using the low-tech tools of pen and paper is the perfect way to interact. Try taking turns writing and passing a notepad back and forth. Choose whether it is to be done in total silence, or if some talking is okay. I have often found that after a period of silence focusing on written information, a natural flow into spoken conversation begins more easily.

NT Agreement #5

Realize that the autistic style of communicating is different from—not inferior nor superior to—the widespread, familiar communication style that you and most neurotypical communicators expect.

Why keep this agreement?

The underlying idea behind the Contract for Communication is to recognize your communication partner's uniqueness as something to understand, rather than judge; to cooperate with, rather than resist; and to respect, rather than extinguish. Recognize that your own communication style is affected by your way of thinking, and how you interpret your experiences. This is one of the ways you and your communication partner are the same—both styles of communication emerge from *how* each of you think.

Not wrong, but different in some ways.

The differences in your communication partner's cognition—in his or her thinking—is the reason you may sometimes be puzzled by unexpected behavior and communication quirks.

Just think, if *you* were on the autism spectrum, then *your thinking* would be different from the majority, and the *way you would understand, interpret, and communicate* would be different than generally expected, too. Not wrong, but different.

This NT Agreement #5 suggests that this shift in attitude is a valuable ingredient toward the goal of improved communication.

The Official NT Agreements

Five agreements to be kept by the neurotypical communication partner

The agreements I have circled below are to be kept by me, _____.

I choose to have authentic, courteous, and mutually considerate communication with
_____, *(name of my communication partner with ASD).*

My Signature _____

Signature of my Communication Partner with ASD _____

NT Agreement #1

I will try to wait quietly during our conversations. I will not expect immediate verbal responses from _____ *(my communication partner with ASD).*

NT Agreement #2

I will try to speak literally and concretely. I will avoid hinting, indirectness, and "chat." I will try to say what I mean, and mean what I say. No more, no less.

NT Agreement #3

I will try to provide information. I will not assume that _____ knows what I think "everyone" automatically knows. When applicable, I will try to use Structured Teaching strategies, Social Stories™, and other helpful strategies.

NT Agreement #4

I will support _____ *(my communication partner with ASD)* in expressing himself or herself with greater ease and authenticity. I will keep communication tools available, such as paper and pen; and access a computer keyboard when helpful. I will try to provide **Communication Forms**, as introduced by the author of this book, which allow _____ *(my communication partner with ASD)* to check and fill in what is true for him/her, in order to facilitate authentic and honest self-expression.

NT Agreement #5

I realize that my communication partner on the spectrum, _____'s style of communicating is different in some ways from—but not inferior to—the widespread, familiar neurotypical style of communication that I am more familiar with and typically expect.

Future Agreements (optional)

As time goes on, we may discover other specific behaviors and/or attitudes that we both have found to be helpful or essential in improving our mutual communication. We may choose to write them down on this contract.

The ASD Agreements

Five specific suggestions for communicators on the spectrum who desire to improve their communication with their NT communication partners are explained in this section. These five suggestions make up the ASD Agreements portion of the Contract for Communication.

This section has been written in the grammatical first person—from the point of view of the reader—for clarity and ease of understanding.

~

Communication leads to community...
to understanding, intimacy and mutual valuing.

—Rollo May

About the ASD Agreements

Some of the suggestions that make up the ASD Agreements may require me to modify how I usually communicate. It takes practice—as most worthwhile endeavors do, but if I try my best to keep my agreements and honor our Contract for Communication, I will more likely succeed in building a stronger connection and a more harmonious relationship with my communication partner.

Every person, ASD or NT, has a unique and distinctive way of communicating. Depending on life circumstances that change from day to day, one or more of the agreements may make a greater impact on improving communication between me and my neurotypical family member, teacher, student, therapist, client, co-worker, employer, employee, friend, etc.

I may discover that there are days when keeping a particular agreement is most helpful; and other days a different agreement is exactly what is needed to keep communication clear.

> I may discover that there are days when keeping a particular agreement is most helpful. On other days a different agreement is exactly what is needed to keep communication clear.

The following section of this book explains the five ASD Agreements.

The author's definitions of the significant terms used in this book can be found in the Glossary.

The official document for signatures is located on pages 33-34.

ASD Agreement #1

I will try to express myself to my communication partner.

Why keep this agreement?

Relationships grow stronger when people feel connected to one another. A way to feel connected to one another is by expressing myself to others and listening to them when they express themselves to me. When I **express myself** to my communication partner, he or she will know and understand me better.

What does it mean to **express myself**?

It means to give information by telling or writing about my thoughts, ideas, needs, fears, hopes, dreams, questions, beliefs, preferences, and/or other things.

Although people often express themselves by talking to one another, there are other methods of communication that sometimes I may prefer.

My communication partner does not automatically know what I think, know, or feel. Each person has his or her own thoughts, ideas, needs, fears, hopes, dreams, beliefs, preferences, etc., but no one knows for sure what they are unless the person expresses them to others. Sometimes people who are in a close relationship with each other may guess, but they do not not know for sure unless they are told.

A way to help my communication partner know me better is to express myself to him or her. Although people often express themselves by talking to one another in conversation, there are other methods of expression. On the next page is a list of ways that I may express myself to my communication partner. **I may choose to do one or more of the following:**

Ask a question. I may ask one or more questions when I need more information or when I am not sure what my communication partner is saying. This is a good way to reveal undetected information. It is a common way to help prevent miscommunication and misunderstanding. (The author suggests that I read her definitions of "miscommunication" and "misunderstanding" in the Glossary.) Questions may be asked by talking; or in written form by writing or typing a note, letter, email, or by responding on a Communication Form.

Take time to think. Respond in a few minutes. I may say to my communication partner, "I need a few more minutes to think about this before I respond. Please wait quietly while I think."

Think about it and respond later. I may say to my communication partner, "I'll think about that and respond later." My communication partner and I may then agree on when we will continue the conversation. It is helpful to write on the day's schedule or on a calendar when it is that we plan to continue to communicate about the topic.

Have a Computer Conversation. I may say to my communication partner, "Let's sit at the computer and communicate quietly by taking turns typing and reading."

Email. I may say to my communication partner, "Let's continue this conversation by email."

Taking turns writing notes with pen and paper. I may say to my communication partner, "Let's communicate about this by taking turns writing on a notepad."

Suggest using a Communication Form with a checklist. I may say, "Please give me a Communication Form with a checklist. I'd like to read and choose from the options."

Suggest using a Communication Form with blanks. I may say, "Please give me a Communication Form with blank lines on which I can fill in by writing (or typing)."

Suggest using a Communication Form with both checklists and blanks. I may say, "Please give me a Communication Form with a checklist and blanks."

Use this page to choose a strategy to try. I may say to my communication partner, "Let's look on this list and choose a way to try communicating."

Offer another alternative. I may have another idea of how I would like to express myself. I'd like to suggest this way to express myself:_____

It helps to know myself...while learning how to express myself.

Getting to know myself is referred to as *self-knowledge*. Self-knowledge is a life-long process for all people. Self-knowledge includes knowing what my skills, strengths, and talents are, as well as my needs. Self-knowledge includes knowing what happiness means to me, what I believe in, how to live a good life, and about being interdependent in my community. Self-knowledge includes identifying when I need help, and asking questions for more information—to advocate for myself.

Because ASD is one thing that makes up who I am, self-knowledge also includes learning more about the autism spectrum and/or Asperger's. Many people learn more by reading books written by authors on the autism spectrum, and by neurotypical authors who care about and work in partnership with people with ASD. Many people with ASD learn more about themselves by meeting and communicating with other people on the spectrum, either in person or on the Internet. It may be helpful for me and my communication partner if I fill out this Communication Form:

☑ I will check what is true for me.

☐ I want to know more about ASD and/or Asperger's. [Circle which one(s).]

☐ I will underline how I would like to get more information, from this list:

Read a book or magazine article.
Go to a website on the Internet.
Listen and talk with my communication partner.
Listen and talk with someone else. *(Name of person, if known:)*_____
Write emails or letters about it with somone. *(Name of person, if known:)* _____
Watch a video.
Another way:_____

☐ I do not want to know more about ASD or Asperger's.

☐ I do not want to know more *now,* but maybe sometime later—in the future.

☐ I am not interested in ASD/Asperger's, but I do want to know more about myself.

☐ I have something to say or ask about this:_____

ASD Agreement #2

I will try to ask for help when I need it. Another term for asking for help is self-advocacy. Sometimes I will try to offer help to my communication partner, too.

Why keep this agreement?

Help means assistance doing or understanding something. Every person needs help sometimes. Asking for help is an important part of communicating. Offering help to others is part of being in a relationship. We are all *interdependent*.

Interdependent means that all people are a part of a family or classroom or school or a particular community or workplace, and in the largest sense, the human race and all of life. We need each other. Wise people say this about life: "We are all in this together."

It is natural to depend on others for certain aspects of life. All people need others for different reasons.

Because of this, it is natural to depend on others for certain aspects of life. Different people need others for different things. Interdependence is a fact of life that can lead to positive connections between people. Needing each other builds community.

In order to ask for help successfully, I must determine the answers to these questions:

1. **WHOM do I ask for help?** (Which person, or which people?)

2. **WHEN and WHERE do I ask for help?** (In which locations, times, activities?)

3. **HOW do I ask for help?** (By talking or writing? In person or another way?)

---

1. WHOM do I ask for help?

My communication partner is a person whom I may ask for help.

My communication partner in this Contract for Communication is:_____

He or she may be the person who will help me in a specific situation, or be able to help me identify who else is able to help in that situation.

If I am supposed to get help from someone else in a certain situation, my communication partner may help me make a plan. I may plan what to say and how to say it, and whether to communicate by talking or by writing. We may also plan what to do in the event of each possible response.

The plan may give specific information to answer these questions: WHOM do I ask for help? WHEN and WHERE do I ask for help? HOW do I ask for help?

2. WHEN do I ask for help?

There are many times when asking for help is the perfect thing to do. Here is a Communication Form about when to ask for help. By filling it out, my communication partner will know more about me.

☑ I will check what is true for me.

A perfect time to ask for help is when I feel confused.

☐ Currently in life, I feel confused. I need more information about something.

☐ I would like more information about:_____

☐ I am not confused currently in my life.

A perfect time to ask for help is when I know what I am supposed to do, but can't seem do it properly.

☐ Currently in my life, there is something I am supposed to do, but I can't seem to do it—either starting to do it, or finishing it.

☐ I need help doing: _____

☐ I do not need help now, but I might need help sometime in the future.

A perfect time to ask for help is when I have tried my best to do something without help, but it just doesn't work out the way I think it should.

☐ Currently in my life, I sometimes do something, but it doesn't work out the way I think it should. It is:_____

☐ Right now, things seems to be working out the way I think they should.

There may be other times when it is perfect to ask for help. My communication partner can help me identify when these times may be in my life. Other perfect times to ask for help are:

☐ _____

☐ _____

☐ _____

☐ _____

---

3. HOW do I to ask for help?

Below is a list of the ways people can ask for help. I may like to experiment with ways to ask for help. I will check the ways that I would like to try sometime.

☐ **Ask my communication partner for help.** I may try to meet with my communication partner in person to ask for help. I may say "Can you please help me with something? I need help with _____."

☐ **Give him/her a note.** I may try to visit or meet with my communication partner with the intent of asking for help. I may write a note and hand it to him or her. The note may say "Can you please help me with _____?"

☐ **Make a phone call.** I may call my communication partner on the phone. He or she may answer, or I may leave a message. I may say, "Hello, this is _____. I am calling to ask if you could please help me with _____. Please respond. My phone number is _____."

☐ **Send an email message.** I may send an email to my communication partner. The message would read "I am writing to ask if you could please help me with _____. Please respond."

☐ **Choose one of the options on page 23 to help me express myself:** When I am with my communication partner, I'll open this book to page 23 and suggest that we try one of the methods listed. I may say to my communication partner, "Let's look on page 23 and choose a way to communicate."

Communication: What Does It Mean to Me?
© 2010 by Catherine Faherty. Future Horizons, Inc.

OFFERING HELP TO MY COMMUNICATION PARTNER:

Everyone needs help sometimes, including my communication partner. I may have a talent or a skill that could be helpful to him or her. Or there may be another kind of help that my communication partner needs.

I may communicate by talking in person, talking on the phone, or writing an email or a letter. In my communication, I may say, "Is there something that I can help you with?"

☑ I will check what is true for me.

☐ I would like to offer help to my communication partner.

☐ I am not sure what kind of help he or she needs, but I am willling to help.

☐ I am not interested in offering help to my communication partner now, but I may in the future.

☐ If my communication partner asks me to help him or her, then I would be willing to help, if it is something I can do.

☐ I am not sure what kind of help I can offer, but I am glad to be of help to my communication partner if he or she asks me.

☐ I do not want, or am unable to help my communication partner at this time.

☐ I have something else to say about this. I want to say_____

ASD Agreement #3

I will try to say "thank you" or write "thank you notes" when someone has helped me, or given me something.

Why keep this agreement?

Saying "thank you" is an expression of gratitude. Gratitude means appreciating things, people, opportunities and events, including the small everyday experiences that make up daily life. Another way of saying thank you is to write a thank-you note. The act of honestly saying "thank you" creates good feeling between people. Feeling and expressing gratitude may help people feel emotionally closer to each other. When I say "thank you" to my communication partner, he or she knows that I appreciate him or her. Most people feel good when they feel appreciated and are thanked. Feeling good may help my communication partner feel emotionally closer to me. My connection with other people may strengthen when I feel and express gratitude to them. Saying "thank you" can be compared to "glue" holding people together.

> Most people feel good when they are thanked. Feeling and expressing gratitude may help people feel emotionally closer to each other.

Researchers are discovering that feeling grateful may also help increase a person's own experience of happiness. Research shows that a person who feels grateful and says "thank you" feels better. Scientists are currently researching the connection between people who feel and express gratitude with that person's own level of happiness.

If I am interested in reading about the latest research on gratitude and how it relates to personal happiness, I can get more information from books written by Ed Diener, Robert Biswas-Diener, Sonja Lyubomirsky, Martin Seligman, and other psychologists who are studying the relationship between gratitude and happiness. Most of this research is in the field of Positive Psychology.

Saying "thank you" can be a simple, but powerful act.

ASD Agreement #4

My communication partner may have different thoughts, ideas, and opinions than mine. This is natural. A first step in understanding him or her better, is to ask about his or her thoughts, ideas, and opinions.

Why keep this agreement?

Understanding and communicating with one another leads to better relationships. The first two ASD Agreements may help improve my relationship with my communication partner by helping him or her understand me better. However, the ASD Agreement #4 will also help me know and understand my communication partner.

People are individuals. The dictionary defines *individual* as "a single human being as distinct from a group, class, or family." Each individual has his or her own experiences in life, which result in developing distinct and sometimes different opinions while growing up. Parents, other family members, teachers, classmates, friends, neighbors, supervisors, and co-workers all may have their own distinct opinions. This is natural.

It is natural for many people, including people on the spectrum—especially young people—to assume that their communication partner (family member, teacher, friend, etc.) has, or should have, the same thoughts, feelings, and/or opinions as they do. In fact, I may assume that my communication partner has the same thoughts, ideas, feelings, and opinions as I do. If this is the case, I may want to find out for sure.

A first step in knowing my communication partner better is to find out his or her thoughts, ideas, feelings, and opinions. Sometimes a person guesses what another person is thinking or feeling based on the other person's actions, words, or what is known about their personal history. However, these are only guesses, and they may not be totally accurate.

> I can know my communication partner's thoughts, ideas, or feelings by asking him or her to tell me what he or she is thinking or feeling. This is accomplished by talking or writing.

Asking my communication partner about his or her thoughts and ideas can be the first step in knowing him or her better.

ASD Agreement #5

I realize that my natural communication style is in some ways different from—not inferior nor superior to—the more widespread neurotypical style of communicating.

Why keep this agreement?

Most people who are on the autism spectrum say that as they grew up they felt different from their peers in ways that seemed beyond the typical differences most people experience. They may have grown up in the time period—not so long ago—when there was no awareness or media coverage, magazine articles, books, Internet sites, or films about ASD or Asperger's. As recently as the late 1990s, the general public rarely heard about autism, and it was still foreign territory for most school teachers. Even now, young people whose ASD has been discovered may not always be provided with accurate, judgment-free information about the spectrum and what it means to them and their relationships. The media seems to focus on how to cure the "autism epidemic" and puts much less attention on how to live a good life with autism. With so much attention on viewing autism as a problem, it is no wonder that a person on the spectrum may feel that he or she is inferior to the larger group of neurotypical people. The truth is that my communication partner and I each have our own style of communication. There are similarities and there are differences in each style, because there are similarities and differences in the ways we think and experience the world. One way is not better nor worse. Our mutual communication can improve when we remember that thinking differently and communicating differently from one another is natural.

> My communication partner and I each have our own style of communication. One style is not better nor worse than the other.

Thinking differently and communicating differently is natural. The Contract for Communication suggests some things that both of us can do to help improve our mutual communication. We are both in this together!

The Official ASD Agreements

Five agreements to be kept by the communication partner with ASD

The agreements I have circled below are to be kept by me, _____.

I choose to have authentic, courteous, and mutually considerate communication with
_____ *(name of my neurotypical communication partner).*

My Signature _____

Signature of my NT Communication Partner _____

ASD Agreement #1

I will try to express myself to _____, *(my NT communication partner).* I will try to share information about my thoughts, needs, fears, hopes, ideas, etc. I will try to remember that _____*(name of my communication partner)* does not automatically know how I think, what I know, or how I feel unless I tell him/her. Using one or more of the ideas on page 23 may help me keep this Agreement #1.

ASD Agreement #2

I will try to ask _____ *(name of my NT communication partner)* for help when there is a need. It is true that everybody needs help sometimes. This is the way of the world. All people are interdependent. I will try to help _____ *(NT communication partner)* , when he/she asks for help from me.

ASD Agreement #3

I will try to remember to say "thank you" or write a "thank you note" when my communication partner, _____ *(name of my NT communication partner)* has helped me, given me something, or otherwise done something for me.

ASD Agreement #4

I will try to remember that sometimes _____ *(name of my NT communication partner)* may have similar thoughts, ideas, and opinions as I do; but other times, _____ *(name of NT communication partner)* may have different thoughts, ideas, and opinions from mine. This is natural. As a first step in knowing and understanding him/her better, I will try to ask him/her about his/her thoughts, feelings, ideas, and opinions. We can communicate by talking and/or writing.

ASD Agreement #5

I realize that my NT communication partner, _____'s style of communicating is in some ways different from—but not superior nor inferior to—the way I communicate.

Future Agreements (optional)

As time goes on, we may discover other specific behaviors and/or attitudes that we both have found to be helpful or essential in improving our mutual communication. We may choose to write them down on this contract.

GLOSSARY

Here are explanations of significant terms in this document, listed in alphabetical order. A dictionary may also be consulted.

Agreement

An arrangement in which people consent to certain conditions, usually relating to their behavior, ideas, and/or attitudes. If people *make an agreement*, it implies that they will try their best to do what they have agreed to do.

ASD

Abbreviation for *Autism Spectrum Disorder*.

Aspie

Slang term for *person with Asperger's*. It was first introduced several years ago by a person on the spectrum.

Autism-friendly

Types of interactions, products, books, events, classrooms, and other community, educational, or family environments that are designed with an understanding of the way people with ASD experience the world. *Autism-friendly* activities are more easily understood by individuals with ASD, and may include modifications in the sensory environment. *Autism-friendly* environments allow greater ease and fuller participation, resulting in more enjoyment for *all* participants—not just one group.

Autism Spectrum Disorder

This is a diagnostic term referring to a broad definition of autism. Individuals with ASD vary widely in ability and personality. Asperger's is an ASD. For everyday use, this author prefers to refer to ASD as *autism spectrum difference*.

Communication

The mutual sharing of ideas, thoughts, feelings, hopes, fears, needs, responses, etc. Communication requires at least two participants, and is a reciprocal activity.

Communication partner

A person who is communicating in the moment, or is in a relationship with another person, thus requiring on-going communication. A communication partner can be a student, teacher, son, daughter, parent, grandparent, cousin, aunt, uncle, spouse, friend, acquaintance, therapist, client, co-worker, supervisor, employee or employer, neighbor, or someone else. They can be NT or ASD.

Communication style

Refers to the *ways* in which people communicate. It includes speech patterns and dialect, but more importantly (for the purposes of this document) it refers to the way people understand others, and the way they express themselves. Specific and unique communicative behaviors and characteristics may be determined by the way an individual thinks, learns, and interprets the world around him or her (cognition). There is a distinct communication style, with beliefs and assumptions about communication among many verbal people on the autism spectrum, just as there are common beliefs and assumptions about communication among their neurotypical communication partners. **These differences between communication styles sometimes result in miscommunication and misunderstanding—the prevention of which is the focus of this book.**

Considerate

Patient, kind, helpful, cooperative, compassionate.

Contract

A verbal or written document agreed upon by two or more people.

Courteous

Polite, well-mannered, considerate, diplomatic.

Miscommunication

Refers to the result when Person #1 tries to communicate something specific to Person #2; but Person #2 doesn't get (misses) what Person #1 is communicating. It is called "mis"communication because Person #2 "misses" what person #1 is trying to communicate. (It can be compared to not catching a ball that is thrown to you.) Or, a miscommunication can happen when Person #1 doesn't realize that the communication was "missed"—unclear or interpreted wrongly by Person #2.

Misunderstanding

This is usually the result of a miscommunication. It is a mix-up, an error, or general confusion resulting from a miscommunication. Person #2 has a different understanding about what Person #1 is communicating. Or, Person #1 thinks that he or she communicated something, and doesn't realize that the communication was unclear or confusing to Person #2. When one communication partner is on the autism spectrum and the other communication partner is neurotypical, a miscommunication and the resulting misunderstanding is often undetected by one or both communication partners. Neither person may realize that there has been a miscommunication or a misunderstanding.

Neurotypical

A current popular term commonly used to describe people who are not on the autism spectrum. It refers loosely (and unscientifically) to those with a *typical neurological system*. The term *neurotypical* was originally suggested by an adult with ASD as a more accurate and descriptive alternative to the word *normal* when describing people not on the autism spectrum. It is used as a label, creating a category for a group of people, just as there is label and category (ASD) to refer to individuals on the autism spectrum. In recent scientific publications with up-to-date research studies, the term *non-spectrum* or *NS* is sometimes used.

NT

Abbreviation for *neurotypical*.

On the spectrum

Refers to individuals who are described as having an autism spectrum disorder (ASD). This includes those who have Asperger's, autism, and those who have been described as having a pervasive developmental disorder (PDD).

Self-advocacy

Refers to a person's act of communicating about himself or herself and his or her needs. *Self-knowledge* and *being able to initiate communication* are two essential ingredients for successful self-advocacy. Sometimes, successful self-advocacy may include educating others about ASD.

Win-win

This is the concept that a particular belief or practice will create a positive result for everyone involved, even if it appears that they are on opposite or conflicting sides, with different needs. *Win-win* is an alternative to the idea that for every winner there has to be a loser. The Contract for Communication is an example of win-win. All of the agreements in the Contract for Communication, whether they are suggested for a person with ASD or their NT communication partner, will benefit both.

APPENDICES

~

The greatest compliment that was ever paid me
was when someone asked me what I thought, and attended to my answers.

—Henry David Thoreau

APPENDIX A:
Helpful Hints for Creating Communication Forms

Engage with Facts

To begin with, you need to *engage* your communication partner by getting him or her interested in using the Communication Form. Dates, times, ages, and other facts are appealing to many children and adults on the spectrum. This is why I often start out with a call for **facts**.

For example, on a Communication Form about the death of a family pet, you may start with having the person list the names and ages of the family's pets, their birthdays, how old they were when the family got them, if the pet is still alive, and the dates of the pets' deaths. For more structure, you can divide another page into columns, with the headings at the top of each column being "Name of Pet," "Birthday," "When we got her," etc. (See the helpful hints under the heading "Sorting and Categorizing" on page 43.) After beginning the Communication Form with facts, then you may continue with additional multiple choice or fill-in-the-blank options. See examples in the Book Excerpts beginning on page 59.

About Multiple Choice

It is sometimes easier for people to look at possible options, and then choose which option matches what they think or feel (rather than having to come up with the wording themselves). Perhaps your communication partner has not yet tried to use words to describe a particular topic, or may not have found the right words to describe an idea, thought, or feeling. Marking "what is true for me" makes it easier to begin to identify an unspoken internal process, and then to describe it in words. It is exciting to witness a person enthusiastically mark what is true, especially when it may be the first time that he or she has identified or communicated a particular thought or feeling in words.

The "Choices" for Multiple Choice

It is imperative that you list a variety of options—including opposing views, as well as differently worded options for what generally would be considered the same answer. Be vigilant about avoiding a tendency to lead the person to what you think the answer should be. Provide real options—even if you *think* you know what he or she will answer. (Many NT communication partners—including parents—are surprised at what they find out about a person they thought they knew well!) Design the form and the number of options to fit the person's age and ability to choose.

Advanced Options for Multiple Choice

Once you are sure that your communication partner understands and can participate in Multiple Choice Communication Forms, you can offer options that may gently and respectfully support the person to expand his or her thinking and life experience. For example, in addition to the choice "I don't want [to do something]" you can present another option that reads "I don't want [to do something] today, but I may want to sometime in the future." Or, "I don't want [to do something] now but if there are good reasons, I may consider [doing it] later." In the case of the last statement, you would then respond with more information, listing and describing what might be considered good reasons. Providing the new information in writing will allow the person to re-read and review it again, later.

Prerequisite to Multiple Choice

You may need to assess if the person can participate by responding accurately to the direction "I will mark what is true for me." Do this by presenting a list of concrete facts about the person you know for sure (age, family facts, likes and dislikes, etc.) and mix the obvious truths amongst obvious false options. For example, for someone whose favorite activity is horsebackriding, one option might be "I like to go horsebackriding," and another option would be "I don't like to go horsebackriding." More information about ways to assess this with examples of Communication Forms can be found in the book *Asperger's ... What Does It Mean To Me?*

Fill-in-the-Blanks

These can be compared to open-ended questions. I will always remember what Dave Spicer (davespicer.org) told me many years ago about open-ended questions. He said that one of the most useless and anxiety-creating questions anyone could ask him when offering free time was, "What do you want to do?" Dave said that in attempting to answer this type of open-ended question, he first had to make a mental list of all the possible things that can be done in that moment (which of course is virtually endless), then evaluate each possibility as realistic or not as a choice in the moment—trying to consider at the same time any rules or expectations; and not until then could he even begin to consider which of the possibilities might be appealing to him. And this whole time, the person who asked the question is standing there, looking at you, impatiently waiting for an answer!

With this in mind, acknowledge the possible difficulty of fill-in-blanks for your communication partner. Fill-in-the-blanks may not give enough information nor the essential structure that allows your communication partner to respond accurately, authentically, or on-topic.Until you know your communication partner's skill, interest, and comfort using Communication Forms, use fill-in-the-blanks sparingly. You can, however, teach *the concept* of fill-in-the-blanks through the consistent use of Communication Forms with multiple choices. See the following page.

Teach the Concept of Fill-in-the-Blanks

A good way to introduce fill-in-the-blanks is to provide an option with a blank line at the end of a list of multiple choices. Because this option comes *after* a list of specific entries within a topic, it helps the person to see the type of information that would be in the category.

On the other hand, your communication partner may have something to say, but not know when, or with whom to express himself. The open-ended blank may allow him to write it down, and even if it is what you would consider "off topic," it may be important for him to say—and important for you to know.

Sorting and Categorizing

This is an uncomplicated, appealing method of helping your communication partner with ASD communicate with you. For many, sorting and categorizing easily focuses their attention on the topic. It is especially helpful as a place to start when you want to introduce or initiate discussion on a new topic.

Draw a line down the center of a piece of paper, and write a category at the top of each column. You can further clarify and limit the open-ended characteristic of possible options by giving each category a finite list of blank lines, open frames, or boxes to be filled in. This method is especially helpful if there is anxiety about the topic, or resistance to the process of communicating. By defining exactly how many responses are needed, it becomes clear that there is an end to the activity—and what it takes to get there.

(See examples in Appendix C on pp. 54-55.)

Try this visual structure of sorting and categorizing when your communication partner needs to reflect on familiar information, consider new information, make decisions, respond to, act on, or otherwise process information for subsequent communication and self-expression.

APPENDIX B:
Sample Communication Forms

Appendix B contains a sampling of Communication Forms and related strategies. They were created for individual children, adolescents, and adults, for a variety of purposes. I offer these to help you get started thinking about Communication Forms you can make for you and your communication partner on the spectrum.

Many of these sample Communication Forms ask for the same type of information, although their visual presentation varies. Each was designed for an individual child or adult. Although they are repetitive in content, I include them to illustrate that Communication Forms are individualized based on the individual's needs, skills, and ability to respond accurately.

You will revise old forms and create new forms for the same person as time goes on, depending on the issues and his or her real-life responses.

Like all effective strategies, the best Communication Forms are those that you create for a particular person, for a particular purpose, at a particular point in time. In our TEACCH Program, we refer to this practice as individualization. Every strategy is restructured to fit an individual person, in a unique situation, at a certain point in time.

How Am I Now?

I will check what is true for me. My teacher will read what I have written. Then my teacher will better understand me and know how to help me have a good day at school.

My favorite thing about today is _____

I'll check what is true for me. I do not have to check everything, only what is true for me, now:

☐ Some work is too hard today.

☐ Some work is easy today.

☐ I feel good.

☐ I am worried.

☐ I feel angry.

☐ I feel something else: _____

☐ There is something that I want to say.

☐ I want _____

How Am I Doing?

I will circle or write what is true for me, so my teachers can better understand me and help me have a good day.

• My favorite work today is _____

• I like _____

• My work is hard today.

• My work is easy today.

• My work is too easy today.

There is something that I'm happy about today. It is:

There is something that I'm worried about today. It is:

There is something that is making me angry today. It is:

Today at Home

I will mark or write what is true for me. My mom or dad will read what I have written. Then he or she will better understand me today.

My favorite thing about today is _____

I'll check what is true for me. I do not have to check everything, only what is true for me, today:

☐ Something is hard today. It is _____

☐ Something is easy today. It is_____

☐ There is something I feel good about. It is _____

_____

☐ There is something I am worried about. It is_____

_____

☐ There is something that makes me angry. It is _____

_____

☐ There is something that I want to say. It is _____

_____

☐ I would like help with _____

I Was Away From Home—Now I Am Back

I was away from home with (circle):

> Mommy
>
> Daddy Bill
>
> Daddy
>
> Memaw
>
> Papaw
>
> Someone else:_____

I was gone from _____ until _____
(I will check the calendar for the dates.)

I did many things. Some things I liked. Some things I did not like.

I liked _____

I did not like_____

When I was gone, I was:
(Circle any that are true.)

Happy. _____made me happy.

Sad. _____made me sad.

Worried. I was worried about _____.

Mad. I was mad about _____.

I want to visit again.   (circle)   YES   or   NO

How and Why to Use this Communication Form at School

A **Communication Form** is a way to let other people know how the day is going for me. Teachers usually do not know what I am thinking or how I am feeling unless I tell them. They do not know my concerns or questions unless I tell them.

Sometimes it is helpful to fill out a **Communication Form** instead of talking directly to a teacher. I can fill out this form and deposit it at the following location:

_____

Mr. Wilshire will pick up this form sometime today and read it. He may want to get more information from me by writing to me, emailing me, or talking to me. Or, he may not need more information.

I will mark (one or more) how I am doing today.   Date/Time:_____

☐ Calm

☐ Secure

☐ Alert

☐ Interested in _____

☐ Happy about _____

☐ Starting to worry about _____

☐ Angry about something. It is _____

☐ Very upset about_____

☐ I feel something else. It is _____

☐ I might need help with something.

☐ I don't know what I need help with.

☐ I **do** know what I need help with. It is _____

☐ I would like to talk with a person I trust.

☐ There is something else I want to communicate. It is _____

How and Why to Use this Communication Form

Sometimes it is helpful to find ways other than always depending on spontaneous speech to tell other people what I need.

A Communication Form is one way to let other people know the general nature of my life at any given time. A Communication Form includes both positive and problematic situations.

Here is the way my **Check-in Communication Form** works:

1. I will read the form, and mark the box beside the statements that are true for me.

2. Next, I give the checklist to _____.
   (This might be my counselor, another professional, or a trusted friend.)

When I give another person my completed Communication Form, he or she will have a general idea of what my current successes and problems are. He or she may want to ask me more questions, in order to learn more about the situation.

Another person does not know most of the events in my life unless I tell him or her.

My Check-in Communication Form

Date: _____

My Feelings:

Overall, I would say that my mood this week has been...

Very Depressed   Neutral   Very Positive

| 1 | 2 | 3 | 4 | 5 | 6 | 7 | 8 | 9 | 10 |

My Current Status:

Recently* I have been concerned about... (check all that apply)

☐ My living situation

☐ My financial situation

☐ My health

☐ Other people's actions

☐ Something at work

☐ My support services (VR, New Vistas, TEACCH, other)

☐ Other _____

* Recently = Within the past month, or since that last time I met with this support team member.

Possible Misinformation Communication Sheet

Date: _____   **Location:** _____

MY TURN: I will describe what I think happened at work:

SUPERVISOR'S TURN: (This middle section is to be filled in by my supervisor to describe in writing, the specific and relevant information about this situation in a clear and literal manner.)

MY TURN: I will mark how I can best communicate right now. (I will check one or more of the choices below.)

☐ I will fill in my At Work Check-In Communication Form.

☐ I will try to answer your questions by writing.

☐ I will try to talk with you in person.

What is easy to do at camp:

What is hard to do at camp:

Things that have been going well since my last session on _____. I do not have to fill in every space, only what is true for me.

Things that have been problems, been upsetting, or that I have concerns about since my last session. I do not have to fill in every space, only what is true for me.

UNDER STRESS

To Whom It May Concern:
(police, fire fighter, paramedics, doctors, etc.)

I have autism. When I am anxious, you may see behavior that could be misinterpreted. Please contact _____ if needed.

I am very literal, so my responses may sound like a joke, but they aren't.
I mean exactly what I am saying.
I may laugh loud and hard, even if there is nothing very funny.
I may not make eye contact with you.
I may be extremely fidgety and restless.
I may pace back and forth.
I may appear to have a bad attitude or I may speak rudely.
I may appear zoned out.
I may not respond to questions.
My responses to your questions may not make sense to you.

(This was co-created with a young woman with ASD, printed, and laminated on an index card. She keeps a copy with her in case she finds herself in a situation in public with police or other first-responders in which she may become anxious. Due to years of learning about ASD and how it affects her and people around her, she was aware that her behavior could be misinterpreted, resulting in our making this card. Since then, other adults with ASD she knows have asked for a similar card. Of course each card is different, based on the individual person's concerns and his or her style of interaction and responses to anxiety.)

Information on Ways to Share during Open Discussion Time in the Social Group

Here is a list of ways to share in the Social Group when it is a person's turn to talk. Group members may choose to refer to this list to help clarify what to do or say when it is their turn. A person may choose to do one or more of the following:

- **Make an announcement.** In this case, the person may have something in particular that he or she wants to announce to the group, but does not want to hear any discussion on the topic. It is simply an announcement. Other group members are invited to listen to the announcement, but not to comment on it. The person who chooses this option must make it clear by saying something like, "I have an announcement, but I am not inviting discussion or comments from anyone. I just have something to announce. I appreciate your listening."

- **Bring up a topic for discussion.** In this case, the person may have a topic that he or she wants to bring up for discussion. The discussion may consist of one or more group members asking questions about the topic. It may also consist of one or more group members sharing their personal opinions about the topic. The person bringing up the topic may say, "I'd like to bring up a topic for discussion." Then introduce the topic. Discussion may follow. For details and information about "discussion" see your User's Guide to the Social Group.

- **Ask a question.** In this case, a person may have something in particular that he or she wants **to ask** one or more group members. In this case, the person who asks the question should make it clear to whom the question is directed. For example, say, "I have a question that I'd like to ask _____. My question is _____."

- Invite **others to ask questions.** In this case, the person may have nothing in particular to say. However, he or she may want to still have a turn to share something about himself or herself. If this is the case, the person may say, "I'm open for questions." Then, usually one or more people will ask him/her one or more questions.

- **Be quiet—pass on a turn to talk.** In this case, the person may want to be at the Social Group, but not want to talk. He or she may want to listen to others, or to simply be in the presence of other group members. He or she may eventually choose to say something, or to ask question—or to stay quiet the whole time. This is okay. It is always an option to be quiet in this group, and to have the option to later decide to say something—or not.

How and Why To Use This Communication Form About My Glasses

A **Communication Form** is a way to let other people know how what I think about something. My parents may not know exactly what I am thinking or how I am feeling unless I tell them. They do not know my thoughts or questions unless I tell them.

Communication Forms can be used for many different things. **This Communication Form is about wearing glasses.** I can check the boxes for the things that are true for me. Then I can give the Communication Form to my mom or dad for them to better understand about me and the glasses. Afterwards, they may want to get more information from me, by talking.

I will check the boxes next to the statements or questions that are true for me. I can check more than one box, if there are more things that are true for me.

☐ *Last year* the eye doctor said that I didn't need glasses.

☐ *This year* the eye doctor said that I need glasses.

☐ I wonder why the eye doctor changed what he said about me needing _____ glasses.

☐ I wonder why I need glasses now, but last year I didn't.

☐ Why do some people need glasses and some people don't need glasses?

☐ I like the way the glasses feel when I wear them.

☐ I do not like the way the glasses feel when I wear them.

☐ The uncomfortable part of the glasses is on my nose.

☐ The uncomfortable part of the glasses is on one or both of my ears.

☐ The uncomfortable part is somewhere else. It is _____.

☐ I would like the eye doctor to give me more information about eyesight, prescriptions, glasses, and contacts.

APPENDIX C:

Excerpts from *Understanding Death and Illness and What They Teach About Life: An Interactive Guide for Individuals with Autism or Asperger's*

The following excerpts are included to demonstrate features introduced in the Contract for Communication. You will find examples of how to communicate in a literal and concrete manner about difficult-to-talk-about topics. In these excerpts, you will see how information is provided in the style of Social Stories™ (www.thegraycenter.org). The reader with ASD is supported and reassured, being given information using the style of communicating as suggested in the **NT Agreements #2** and **#3**.

These excerpts also demonstrate the extensive use of Communication Forms to help a person explore their own thoughts and ideas, connect with others, and practice self-advocacy. These features directly correspond to the Contact for Communication as suggested in **NT Agreements #1** and **#4**, and **ASD Agreements #1** and **#2**.

In these excerpts, notice how Communication Forms can help a person (1) identify his or her own ideas, thus encouraging self-knowledge; (2) express himself or herself to others, thus helping build relationships; (3) communicate the need for more information, and/or help, thus laying the foundation for developing self-advocacy skills, and (4) be introduced to new concepts in a straightforward manner, thus expanding thinking and experiences.

These excerpts are taken from various chapters of the workbook, *Understanding Death and Illness and What They Teach About Life: An Interactive Guide for Individuals with Autism or Asperger's and their Loved Ones* (Future Horizons, 2008), by Catherine Faherty and illustrated by Thomas Johnson. It was awarded the **2009 Autism Society of America's Outstanding Literary Work of the Year in the Family/Social Division.** However it is not just about illness, death, and dying. It demonstrates the interconnectedness of living and dying by introducing concepts that come to the forefront when people face death. It encourages the reader to reflect on his or her own life and offers simple, positive guidelines for living.

The first selections specifically address communication:

- What is communication?

- Why is communication important?

- What are the most common methods of communication?

- How do people communicate effectively?

- What is a miscommunication?

- What should be done in cases of miscommunication?

- Why is understanding each other so important?

- Understanding goes two ways

- What is other important information about communicating?

The next selections explain how certain character traits and choices can help people lead happier lives and make those around them happier as well:

- Appreciation and Gratitude

- Self-knowledge

- Courage

- Respect

- Kindness

- Honesty

- The Combination of Honesty, Respect, and Kindness

Finally, the last excerpts address issues related to death in a positive, concrete way:

- How do people or animals die?

- What does it mean when someone dies after being sick or injured?

- Where do people die?

- Where do animals die?

- What does it mean when a pet has to be "put to sleep"?

- Do doctors put people "to sleep" in the same way as veterinarians put animals "to sleep"?

- What does it mean to "live one day at a time"?

Excerpts   62-93

Table of Contents   94-99

What is communication?

Communication is an action that allows one person (or group of people) to know and understand what another person (or group of people) is thinking or feeling. Communication is how people share ideas from one mind to another mind.

The act of communication is most frequently accomplished through talking or writing.

There are many other ways to communicate—through art, music, dance, and other art forms.

Another person (or group of people) receives the communication by hearing or reading or seeing or sensing what is being communicated.

In order for communication to be successful, the person **receiving** the communication must understand what is being communicated.

Communication: What Does It Mean to Me?
© 2010 by Catherine Faherty. Future Horizons, Inc.

Communication Form
☑ I will check what is true for me.

☐ I will circle the ways in which I sometimes communicate:

- Talking face-to-face with another person
- Talking by phone
- Writing and sending emails
- Writing and mailing letters by post
- Manual sign language
- Using pictures or picture symbols
- Drawing or painting
- Computer graphics
- Singing
- Playing a musical instrument
- Dance or creative movement
- Writing stories or essays
- Writing poetry
- Other art form: _____
- Talking about or showing someone things that I like
- Other: _____
- Other: _____
- It is usually easiest for me to communicate by the following method(s):

_____

_____

☐ I have something to say or questions to ask: _____

_____

Why is communication important?

Communication is often the first step in understanding one another. It is a direct way for people to connect with one another.

No one really knows what thoughts are in someone else's mind, or what feelings are in someone else's heart, unless the thoughts, ideas, or feelings are communicated.

Communication is considered by many people to be one of the most important activities in which a person can participate because it is a way to build connections with others.

Communication can help us understand one another. It can contribute to a more peaceful life.

Communication Form
☑ I will check what is true for me.

☐ There is something that people should understand about me. They should understand that _____

_____

☐ I want to understand more about something or someone. I would like to understand more about _____

_____

☐ I have something to say or questions to ask: _____

_____

What are the most common methods of communication?

Communication can be verbal (talking and listening) or visual (writing and reading).

A person who has something to communicate can talk, write a letter with pen or pencil, or use a computer.

If it is written, it can be on paper, on the computer and printed out, or by email.

Some people communicate by gesturing with their hands. They may communicate using facial expressions and eye contact. Some people may use pictures or photographs to communicate.

The most common methods are talking and listening, writing and reading.

Communication Form
☑ I will check what is true for me.

☐ I will mark the words in the paragraph above that describe the ways I prefer to communicate.

☐ I do not know how I prefer to communicate.

☐ I have questions or something to say: _____

_____

How do people communicate effectively?

When people communicate effectively, they talk to another person at a time when the other person is able to pay attention and listen carefully. Or they write it and make sure that the other person receives the letter or message.

It is often necessary to make sure that the other person understands what is being said (or what was written). The speaker (or writer) may ask, **"Do you understand what I said?"** or **"Do you understand what I have written?"** If the person does not understand, then more information can be said or written.

Another part of communication is listening and trying to understand what someone else is saying. If the communication is written, the other person must be able to read and comprehend what has been written.

What is a miscommunication?

When a person tries to communicate, but other people are confused about what was said or written, it can be considered a **miscommunication.**

If what is being communicated doesn't make sense to the listener or the reader, it can be considered a **miscommunication**.

What should be done in cases of miscommunication?

After noticing that there may be a miscommunication, the listener may politely request that the speaker **"please explain it again."** This is an intelligent and responsible thing to do when something is confusing or doesn't make sense.

Another option is for the listener to politely request that the speaker **"please write it down to make sure I understand."** Asking for more explanation in written form is an intelligent and responsible thing to do.

Sometimes other people may say that they don't understand what I am saying. This may also be an example of miscommunication. If someone asks me to explain it again, it means that the listener or reader needs more information in order to better understand what I am saying.

It is intelligent and responsible to try to ask for—and to give—more information by talking or writing.

Communication Form
☑ I will check what is true for me.

☐ I prefer to communicate by talking.

☐ I prefer to communicate by writing.

☐ I would like to have a choice when communicating, sometimes talking, sometimes writing, sometimes listening, and sometimes reading.

☐ There are times when I do not understand what is being communicated.

☐ Sometimes I would like to **read** what a person is saying to me.

☐ When I don't understand, I usually am quiet. I usually don't say anything.

☐ When I don't understand, I usually ask the person to explain.

☐ I usually understand these people best:_____

☐ I have trouble understanding these people:_____

☐ I think that these people understand me best: _____

☐ These people usually don't understand me:_____

☐ I have something to say or questions to ask: _____

_____

Why is understanding each other so important?

"Misunderstanding" means **not** understanding.

"Miscommunication" means that there is a problem with a specific attempt at communication.

Misunderstanding and miscommunication between people can be compared to there being thick walls between people. Thick walls between people would make it difficult for people to see, hear and, therefore, understand each other.

Understanding can be compared to the thick walls coming down between people.

When the "walls" are down, people are able to "see" each other more clearly. They are able to listen to each other. They may begin to understand each other better.

They may find out that even though people are different from one another, there are some ways that people are the same. Sometimes they discover that they have ideas, thoughts, dreams, desires, fears, feelings, or other experiences in common.

They may also learn to accept that there are differences between people. They may learn to respect other human beings, even though there are differences.

When people understand and/or respect each other, individual lives and society in general may improve.

One pathway to greater understanding is communication.

Communication Form
☑ I will check what is true for me.

☐ I think there is a misunderstanding or a miscommunication between me and someone else.

☐ There often are misunderstandings or miscommunications between me and someone else.

☐ The person or people I have misunderstandings or miscommunications with are: _____

_____

☐ I am not sure what is meant by "misunderstanding."

☐ I am not sure what is meant by "miscommunication."

☐ I have questions or something to say: _____

_____

"Understanding" Goes Two Ways:

Trying to understand someone else is a necessary part of communication.

There are a lot of people in the world, and there are many different beliefs and opinions.

Even when there is a disagreement, it is important to try to understand one another.

It takes strength of character to try to understand someone who has a different opinion.

Communication Form

☑ I will check what is true for me.

☐ There is something that I want to understand. It is: _____

_____

☐ There is someone whom I want to understand better. The person is
(name)_____

☐ I want other people to understand something about me. It is: _____

_____

☐ I have questions or something to say: _____

_____

What is other important information about communication?

Successful communication is done honestly and with respect. Both of these qualities (honesty and respect) are what make a successful communicator.

Being honest is saying what is true for oneself.

Being respectful is acting courteously and politely.

Communicating in a respectful manner is of utmost importance. Positive change is possible when communication is both honest and respectful. Connections with people may be strengthened when communication is both honest and respectful. More information can be found in Chapter 16.

Communication Form
☑ I will check what is true for me.

☐ I understand what it means to be honest.

☐ I do not understand what it means to be honest.

☐ I understand what it means to be respectful.

☐ I do not understand what it means to be respectful.

☐ I understand what it means to be courteous or polite.

☐ I do not understand what it means to be courteous or polite.

☐ I think that I am usually honest. I say what it true for me.

☐ I think that I am usually respectful. I usually am courteous and polite.

☐ I am not sure if I am usually both honest and respectful when I communicate.

☐ I would like more information about honesty, respect, and being polite.

Appreciation and Gratitude

To appreciate means to cherish and value something. Gratitude means thankfulness. People may appreciate and be grateful for things, ideas, people, opportunities, events, experiences, and life itself.

Many people realize that it is important to be grateful for the little things that happen each day.

When facing death, many people become grateful for things that they usually don't notice, like clean air to breathe, or a warm house when it is cold outside, or good food to eat, or a functional computer, or a family member who cares for them. They begin to appreciate what they have experienced in life.

They may choose to say "thank you" to certain people who are important to them. They may choose to say "thank you" for life.

Communication Form
☑ I will check what is true for me.

☐ I appreciate my life.

☐ I am grateful for certain things in my life. Some of these things are _____

_____

☐ I am grateful for certain people in my life. The names of some of these people are: _____

☐ I would like to say thank you to the following people: _____

_____

☐ I would like to start a **Gratitude Journal**. It is a special book in which to write lists of things I am grateful for. Before going to bed, I may write one or more things that I or did or saw or otherwise experienced that day … things that I am grateful for.

☐ I would like to start a list of things I am grateful for, like a **Gratitude Journal,** but I would like to keep the list on a computer, instead of in a book. I could create a new document called **Gratitude Journal** on the desktop of the computer.

☐ I do not understand what it means to appreciate or to be grateful.

☐ I would like more information about this subject.

☐ I have questions or something to say about this:_____

_____

Self-Knowledge

As people grow from childhood to adolescence to adulthood, they learn more about themselves. The result of "getting to know yourself" is called "self-awareness" or "self-knowledge."

The process of gaining self-knowledge continues throughout life.

People may learn about their strengths, skills, and interests. They may learn about their challenges.

They may learn to observe how they react in different situations. They may learn to observe how they feel and what they think.

They may learn about how to improve themselves. They may learn better ways of reacting and thinking. They may learn how to communicate clearly, and how to understand others better.

They may learn to ask for help. They may learn to offer help to others.

They may learn how to live a good life. They may discover their unique purpose in life.

The process of self-knowledge continues throughout life.

Communication Form
☑ I will check what is true for me.

☐ I am learning more about myself.

☐ Some of the things I do well are _____

_____

☐ Some of my interests are _____

_____

☐ Things that are challenging to me are _____

_____

☐ I would like help with the following things: _____

_____

☐ I am able to help others with the following things:_____

_____

☐ I will highlight or underline sentences on the previous page that are
    interesting to me.

☐ I would like to learn more about myself.

☐ I would like to understand myself better.

☐ I would like other people to understand me better.

☐ I have questions or something to say: _____

_____

Courage

Courage is the quality of mind or spirit that helps a person face fear or uncertainty with confidence. Courage helps a person do what may seem too difficult or impossible to accomplish. Instead of giving up, a person can choose to have courage.

With courage, a person can accomplish more than he or she thinks. Courage is the antidote to fear.

Every person needs courage to live in the world.

It takes courage to do things that feel difficult to do.

Sometimes it takes courage to talk to other people.

It takes courage to learn about oneself, to accept some things, to learn about oneself, and to communicate.

Every person can choose to have courage in his or her life.

With courage, a person can feel confident to try new things. Choosing courage and trying what seems difficult helps a person become stronger and wiser.

Courage helps a person learn and grow to be a better person.

Communication Form

☑ I will check what is true for me.

☐ I understand what courage is.

☐ I want to understand about courage.

☐ Sometimes I feel afraid about_____

_____

☐ I would like to have courage about_____

_____

☐ There have been times when I have chosen to have courage.

☐ It took courage for me to do or say certain things. This is what I did or
said that required courage:_____

_____

_____

☐ If I had courage, then it would be easier for me to do or say these things:

_____

_____

☐ I have questions or something to say: _____

_____

_____

Respect

Respect is being polite and courteous to others.

Being respectful is a mature way to relate to others.

Children, parents, family members, teachers, friends, and others have better relationships when they respect each other.

Respect for others and for oneself helps people work, play, and live better with each other.

Communication Form

☑ I will check what is true for me.

☐ I usually try to be polite and courteous to others.

☐ I am not sure if I am polite and courteous to others.

☐ I think I am usually respectful to others.

☐ I am not sure if I am respectful to others.

☐ I try to be respectful with certain people. They are: _____

_____

☐ I feel respected by others.

☐ I think that (names) _____ respect me.

☐ I do not feel respected by others.

☐ I think that (names) _____ may not respect me.

☐ I would like more information about respect.

Communication: What Does It Mean to Me?
© 2010 by Catherine Faherty. Future Horizons, Inc.

Kindness

Kindness is the quality of being pleasant and friendly. Kind actions are based on concern for others.

Being kind is another way for people to make daily life better for themselves and others.

An act of kindness toward another person can change a bad day into a good day—for both people. Kindness helps people feel good.

Sometimes when people are dying they may remember acts of kindness that were directed toward them in their lives.

Kindness is a gentle but powerful act.

Communication Form
☑ I will check what is true for me.

☐ I usually try to be pleasant and friendly.

☐ I am not sure if I am pleasant and friendly.

☐ Some people are friendly to me. They are (names):_____

☐ Some people are not friendly to me. If I know their names, I may write them here: _____.

☐ Most people are friendly to me.

☐ No one is friendly to me.

☐ I remember a time when someone was kind to me. What this person did:

_____

_____

☐ I remember a time when I was kind to someone else. What I did: _____

_____

_____

☐ I would like more information about kindness.

☐ I have questions or something to say: _____

_____

Honesty

Being honest is an important trait. It means telling the truth. It means saying what is true for oneself. Good communication depends on honesty and truthfulness.

Honesty comes naturally to some people, especially many children and adults with ASD.

Honesty is an honorable trait.

The Combination of Honesty, Respect, and Kindness

Sometimes people who are honest all the time may unintentionally hurt other people's feelings.

Sometimes hearing certain types of true statements may embarrass people. Some statements about a person's appearance or other personal information may feel hurtful to the person.

People may say that their "feelings are hurt." They may feel so hurt that they may misunderstand what is being communicated. They may think that the honest person is trying to be cruel to them or is too critical.

It is often possible to be honest without hurting someone's feelings. The way to do this is to say what is true while speaking respectfully and kindly. Or learning not to say certain things is respectful and kind in some situations.

It is possible to learn to be honest, respectful, and kind at the same time. It is a communication skill.

Honesty that is tempered with kindness and respect is an honorable trait.

Communication Form
☑ I will check what is true for me.

☐ I usually am honest and truthful.

☐ I tell the truth all the time.

☐ Sometimes I do not tell the truth.

☐ I don't know if I usually am honest and truthful.

☐ I don't know if I have hurt someone's feelings by being honest.

☐ It is possible that I may have hurt someone's feelings by being honest.

☐ I think (name) _____'s feelings were hurt when I said this:

_____

_____

☐ My feelings were hurt when (name)_____said something
to me. What was said to me: _____

_____

_____

☐ I am not sure how to be honest, respectful, and kind at the same time.

☐ I would like more information about how to be honest, respectful, and
kind at the same time.

☐ I have questions or something to say: _____

_____

How do people or animals die?

Generally there are three different ways of dying.

1. Some people and animals die after a period of time of sickness or injury.

2. Some people and animals die suddenly and unexpectedly.

3. Some people and animals die after they have lived a long life and are old.

More information about these three ways of dying is given in this chapter.

What does it mean when someone dies after being sick or injured?

One way of dying is when a person or animal has been sick or injured.

An illness may be so severe that it causes the dying process to begin.

Or if a person was injured in an accident, the injury may be so severe that it causes the dying process to begin.

When people say that someone is dying, it is understood that the person or animal may die soon, possibly within the year.

Usually no one is sure exactly how soon the person will die. Doctors and nurses have been with many people and animals who have been sick or injured and then died, so they may be able to guess when the person might die. It might be in hours, days, weeks, or months. But they are just making an educated guess.

No one knows for sure until the person or animal actually dies. Sometimes doctors and family members are surprised if the person dies sooner than they had guessed. Other times the person takes a long time to die. Sometimes a person may be dying for many months or years.

Communication Form

☑ I will check what is true for me.

☐ I know a person or animal who is dying because of being sick. His or her name is _____

☐ I know someone who is probably dying because he or she was in an accident. His or her name is _____

☐ I know someone who is probably dying after he or she has lived a long life and is very old. His or her name is_____

☐ If a person or people in my life have already died, I will write their names, with the date and approximate time of death here: _____

_____

_____

☐ If animals in my life have already died, I will write their names, with the date and approximate time of death here: _____

_____

_____

☐ I have something to say or questions to ask: _____

_____

Where do people die?

People may die in different locations. They may be at home or somewhere else.

In some countries, elderly people sometimes live in a special home because they need help taking care of themselves. They may die in this special home.

Sometimes people who have been dying for a while may be in a Hospice facility where people are taken care of to help them die peacefully. Hospice is the name of an organization that specializes in helping people die peacefully.

In the case of accidents, a person may die at the site of the accident, in an ambulance or in a hospital. Or a person may die somewhere else.

Communication Form
☑ I will check what is true for me.

☐ I know someone who has died. I wonder where he or she was at the moment of death.

☐ I know where he or she was at the moment of death. Location:

_____

☐ I know someone who is dying. I wonder where he or she wants to be at the moment of death.

☐ I want more information about this topic.

☐ I want to talk with my parents or a trusted friend or support person about this topic.

☐ I have something to say, or questions to ask: _____

_____

Where do animals die?

Animals may die in different locations.

They may be inside, at home. They may be at the veterinarian's office. They may be outside.

In the case of an accident, the animal may die at the site of the accident, or nearby.

Some animals who are very sick or very injured may want to be alone. Some animals find a quiet place to lie down and die peacefully.

Some animals may want to be near other animals or people when they are dying.

Communication Form
☑ I will check what is true for me.

☐ I knew an animal who died.

☐ I know where he or she was at the moment of death. The location was:

_____

☐ I know an animal who is dying. I wonder where he or she will be at the moment of death.

☐ I want more information about this topic. I want to talk with my parents or a trusted friend or support person about this topic.

☐ I have something to say, or questions to ask: _____

_____

What does it mean when a pet has to be "put to sleep"?

Sometimes dogs or cats or other pets become very sick. Or they are very very old.

An animal might not be able to walk or eat, or it may be feeling a lot of pain. It may make sounds, or it may be very quiet. The veterinarian may think that the animal is hurting inside its body.

The veterinarian may understand that the animal will never get better again; that the animal is dying.

Sometimes the most helpful thing to do for an animal that is loved by its family is to "put him or her to sleep." This is the term used to describe the way the veterinarian and family members help animals die peacefully when they are coming close to the end of their lifespan.

"Putting an animal to sleep" does not mean that it is going to sleep in the usual way. It will not really sleep and wake up. An animal that has been "put to sleep" in this way does not wake up.

It does not hurt the animal to be "put to sleep." It is usually considered to be a humane and compassionate way to help animals die easily and without pain. It is a legal method performed by veterinarians using special drugs and injections. It takes only minutes for the animal to die peacefully. Another name for this is "euthanasia."

Communication Form
☑ I will check what is true for me.

☐ An animal or several animals are a part of our family. The names and ages of the animals are: _____

_____

_____

☐ I know an animal (or animals) who have died. Their names and the dates of their deaths are: _____

_____

_____

☐ I have never had a pet who has died.

☐ I wonder if our pet is sick or injured.

☐ I wonder if our pet may die soon.

☐ I wonder if we will help our pet die peacefully by having the veterinarian put him or her to sleep.

☐ I want to talk with a trusted person and/or the veterinarian about this.

☐ I have something to say or questions to ask: _____

_____

Do doctors put people "to sleep" in the same way as veterinarians put animals "to sleep"?

No, generally they do not. Most people in the world die naturally because of old age, illness, or accidents.

Once in a while a person who has been dying for a long time feels lots of pain. There may be no medicine or treatment that relieves the severe pain. The person may ask the doctor to prescribe the drugs that will cause unconsciousness and cause the body to stop functioning, making death happen soon.

All doctors, families, religions, and government officials do not agree on whether this should be a choice for humans. Most people agree that it is different for animals. It is common for veterinarians to help animals die peacefully.

Doctors giving people drugs to cause death in this way is rare. It is illegal in many parts of the world. Euthanasia for people is controversial. This means that many people have strong feelings about it.

Some people feel strongly that euthanasia should be a choice for people who are dying and in severe pain.

Other people feel strongly that it is wrong to help someone die in this way. Some religions have strong opinions on euthanasia.

Some people become very upset by this topic. Some people may not want to talk about it at all.

If a person has questions or opinions about euthanasia, he or she should talk with family members or others about it at home, privately, and at a time when a person who is sick and/or dying is not present. Talking about it privately is polite and respectful.

Euthanasia is a topic that may be upsetting for some people to hear about or to talk about.

Communication Form

☑ I will check what is true for me.

☐ I wonder about my family's opinion on euthanasia. I have something to say or questions to ask. My questions are: _____

_____

_____

☐ If I have a religion, I wonder what our religious beliefs are about this topic.

☐ I want to talk with a priest, minister, pastor, rabbi, cleric, teacher, or other religious offical about this topic.

☐ I have a question about euthanasia.

☐ I have an opinion about euthanasia.

☐ I do not have an opinion about euthanasia.

☐ I want to talk with someone about euthanasia. The person or people I want to talk with are _____

_____

☐ I have something to say or questions to ask: _____

_____

What does it mean to "live one day at a time"?

This suggests that people are to think about the present moment, with their full attention on … now. Another way to say this is to "be here now." It is also stated as "being present."

It is good to have future goals to work toward; however, it is also very important to experience the present moment, each day, and to live one day at a time.

It can be compared to walking upstairs. When walking upstairs, people must take one step at a time. Eventually they come to the top.

But on the way up, they must keep their attention on each step they take, one by one, or they may fall.

Each single step can be compared to living each single day, one day at a time. Step by step. Day by day.

The idea of "living one day at a time" is to keep our attention on what is happening right now. It reminds us to experience life in the present moment.

It means to do the best you can do, now, one step at a time.

Communication Form
☑ I will check what is true for me.

☐ I am interested in understanding more about what it means to "live one day at a time."

☐ I worry about the future. If this is true, I can try to do the following:

- Check the schedule for the day.

- Check the calendar for the week or month.

- Ask someone to help me write in the schedule or calendar the events that are coming up. Write the answers to my questions about "When will _____ happen?"

- After checking and writing on the schedule and calendar, try to remember to "be present" and do my best today, moment by moment.

☐ I sometimes worry about something specific in the future. I sometimes worry about_____

_____

☐ I want to learn more about "living one day at a time."

☐ I have something to say or questions to ask: _____

_____

The Table of Contents from *Understanding Death and Illness and What They Teach about Life*

What are the most common methods of communication? 88

What is other important information about communication? 89

If there is something that a person didn't communicate to someone who died, is it too late now? 90

CHAPTER 6: What Happens to the Person Who Dies **93**

What does it mean that death is a "mystery"? 94

What happens to the person after he or she dies? 95

What do "belief" and "to believe in something" mean? 95

What are some beliefs about what happens to the person after death? 96

Most people agree on one thing 98

CHAPTER 7: Putting Pets To Sleep **101**

What does it mean when a pet has to be "put to sleep"? 102

Do doctors put people "to sleep" in the same way as veterinarians put animals "to sleep"? 104

CHAPTER 8: Rituals and Traditions **107**

What rituals and traditions are practiced after someone has died? 108

What is a "wake" or a "viewing"? 110

What is a closed casket, and an open casket? 112

What is a funeral service? 114

What is a graveside service? 116

What is a memorial service? 118

What is a "celebration of life" for someone who has died? 120

What happens when people come to a family member's home after a service? 121

CHAPTER 9: Taking Care of the Physical Body **123**

What happens to the body after dying? 124

What is a shroud? 124

What does it mean for the body to be buried? 126

What is a cemetery? 128

What are tombs, crypts, and mausoleums? 130

What does it mean to be "buried at sea"? 131

What does it mean for the body to be cremated? 132

What happens to the cremains? 132

What does it mean for the body to be donated to science? 134

Does being cremated, buried, kept in a mausoleum, or being
    donated to science, hurt the person who has died? 136

Who decides what to do with the body? 136

CHAPTER 10: What People Say and Do **139**

What do people say after someone has died? 140

What should I say if someone tries to say "comforting words" to me? 142

What if someone tries to touch, hug, or kiss me at this time? 142

CHAPTER 11: Taking Care of the Soul: More Rituals and Traditions **145**

Why do people visit the grave, shrine, or keep the cremains of the person who has died? 146

Why do people sometimes do special things to remember the person who has died? 148

Does everyone have to participate in a special ritual for someone who has died? 148

For more information about this title, visit the Future Horizons website at www.FHautism.com.

SUPPORTIVE RESEARCH

Agosta, E., Graetz, J. E., Mastropieri, M. A. & Scruggs, T. E. (2004). "Teacher-researcher partnerships to improve social behaviour though social stories." *Intervention in Schools and Clinic* 39 (5) 276 – 287.

Bryan, L. C., & Gast, D. L. (2000). Teaching on-task and on-schedule behaviors to high-functioning children with autism via picture activity schedules. *Journal of Autism and Developmental Disorders,* 30, 553-567.

Chalk M. (2003). Social stories for adults with autism and learning difficulties. *Good Autism Practice* 4(2), pp. 3-7.

Del Valle, P. R., McEachern, A. G. & Chambers, H. D. (2001). "Using social stories with autistic children." Journal of Poetry Therapy 14 (4) 187-197.

Dettmer, S., Simpson, R. L., Myles, B.S., & Ganz, J. B. (2000). The use of visual supports to facilitate transitions of students with autism. *Focus on Autism and Other Developmental Disabilities,* 15, 163-169

Dooley, P., Wilczenski, F. L., & Torem, C. (2001). Using an activity schedule to smooth school transitions. *Journal of Positive Behavior Interventions,* 3, 57-61.

Erangey, K. (2001). "Using social stories as a parent of a child with an ASD." *Good Autism Practice* 2 (1) 309-323.

Gastgeb, H.Z., Strauss, M.S., & Minshew, N.J. (2006). "Do individuals with autism process categories differently? The effect of typicality and development." *Child Development* 77, 1717–1729.

Gray, C. (2004). "Social stories 10.0: The new defining criteria and guidelines." *Jenison Autism Journal* 15, 2–21.

Gray, C.A. & Garand, J.D. (1993). "Social stories: Improving responses of students with autism with accurate social information." *Focus on Autistic Behavior* 8, 1–10.

Gray, C. (1998a). "Social stories and comic strip conversations with students with Asperger syndrome and high functioning autism." In: E. Schopler, G. Mesibov & L. Kunce (Eds.). *Asperger syndrome or high functioning autism?* (pp. 167-198). New York: Plenum Press.

Howley, M. (2001). "An investigation into the impact of social stories on the behaviour and social understanding of four pupils with autistic spectrum disorder." In R. Rose and Grosvenor (Eds) (2001). *Doing research in special education.* London: David Fulton.

Howley, M.,& Arnold,E. (2005). *Revealing the hidden social code.* London: Jessica Kingsley.

Hume, K., & Odom, S. (2007). Effects of an individual work system on the independent functioning of students with autism. *Journal of Autism and Developmental Disorders,* 37(6), 1166-1180.

Hutchins, Tiffany L., & Prelock, Patricia A. (2008). Supporting theory of mind development: Considerations and recommendations for professionals providing services to individuals with autism spectrum disorder. *Topics in Language Disorders,* 28, 340-364.

Iovannone, R., Dunlap, G., Huber, H., & Kincaid, D. (2003). Effective educational practices for students with autism spectrum disorders. *Focus on Autism and other Developmental Disabilities,* 18, 150-165.

Ivey, M.L., Heflin, L.J., & Alberto, P. (2004). "The use of social stories to promote independent behaviors in novel events for children with PDD-NOS (autism spectrum disorder)." *Focus on Autism and Other Developmental Disabilities* 19, 164–176.

Kamio, Y., & Toichi, M. (2000). Dual access to semantics in autism: Is pictorial access superior to verbal access? *Journal of Child Psychology and Psychiatry,* 41, 859-868.

Klinger, L.G., & Dawson, G. (2001). "Prototype formation in autism." *Development and Psychology* 13, 111–124.

Kuoch, H., & Mirenda, P. (2003). "Social story interventions for young children with autism spectrum disorders." *Focus on Autism and Other Developmental Disorders* 18, 219–227.

Kuttler, S., Myles, B. S., & Carlson, J. K. (1998). "The use of social stories to reduce precursors to tantrum behaviour in a student with autism." *Focus on Autism and Other Developmental Disabilities* 12, 176-182.

Lorimer, P. A., Simpson, R., Myles, B. S. & Ganz, J. (2002). "The use of social stories as a preventative behavioral intervention in a home setting with a child with autism." *Journal of Positive Behavioral Interventions* 4 (1) 53-60.

Mesibov, G. B., Browder, D. M., & Kirkland, C. (2002). Using individualized schedules as a component of positive behavioral support for students with developmental disabilities. *Journal of Positive Behavioral Interventions, 4,* 73-39.

Mesibov, G. B., Howley, M. (2003). Accessing the curriculum for pupils with autistic spectrum disorders: using the TEACCH programme to help inclusion. London: David Fulton Publishers.

Mesibov, G. B., & Shea, V. (2009). Evidence-based practices and autism. *Autism: The International Journal of Research and Practice.* (in press).

Mesibov, G. B., Shea, V., & Schopler, E. (with Adams, L., Burgess, S., Chapman, S. M., Merkler, E., Mosconi, M., Tanner, C., & Van Bourgondien, M.E.). (2005). *The TEACCH approach to autism spectrum disorders.* New York: Springer.

Mesibov, G. B., & Stephens, J. (1990). Perceptions of popularity among a group of high-functioning adults with autism. **Journal of Autism and Developmental Disorders**, 20(1), 33-43.

Moffat, E. (2001). "Writing social stories to improve students' social understanding." *Good Autism Practice* 2 (1) 12-16.

National Research Council. (2001). *Educating children with autism.* Committee on Educational Interventions for Children with Autism. Division of Behavioral and Social Sciences and Education. Washington, DC: National Academy Press.

Norris, C., & Dattilo, J. (1999). "Evaluating the effects of social story intervention on a young girl with autism." *Focus on Autism and Other Developmental Disabilities* 14, 180-186.

O'Riordan, M. A., Plaisted, K.C., Driver, J., & Baron-Cohen, S. (2001). Superior visual search in autism. *Journal of Experimental Psychology*, 27, 719-730.

Panerai, S., Ferrante, L., & Zingale, M. (2002). Benefits of the treatment and education of autistic and communication handicapped children (TEACCH) programme as compared with a non-specific approach. *Journal of Intellectual Disability Research*, 46, 318-327.

Quill, K. A. (1997). Instructional considerations for young children with autism: The rationale for visually cued instruction. *Journal of Autism and Developmental Disorders*, 27, 697-714.

Rowe, C. (1999). "Do social stories benefit children with autism in mainstream primary school?" *British Journal of Special Education* 26 (1), 12-14.

Sansosti, F.J., Powell-Smith, K.A., & Kincaid, D. (2004). "A research synthesis of social story interventions for children with autism spectrum disorders." *Focus on Autism and Other Developmental Disabilities* 19(4), 194–204.

Sarokoff, R. A., Tayler, B. A., & Poulson, C. L. (2001). Teaching children with autism to engage in conversational exchanges: Script fading with embedded textual stimuli. *Journal of Applied Behavioral Analysis*, 34, 81-84.

Scattone, D., Wilczynski, S., Edwards, R. & Rabian, B. (2002). "Decreasing disruptive behaviors of children with autism using social stories." *Journal of Autism and Developmental Disorders* 32 (6) 535-543.

Smith, C. (2001a). "Using social stories to enhance behaviour in children with autistic spectrum difficulties." *Educational Psychology in Practice* 17, (4) 337-345.

Smith, C. (2001b). "Using social stories with children with autistic spectrum disorders: An evaluation." *Good Autism Practice* 2 (1) 16-25.

Sperry, L. A. & Mesibov, G. B. (2005). Perceptions of social challenges of adults with autism spectrum disorder. *Autism: The International Journal of Research and Practice*, 9(4), 362-376.

Stromer, R., Kimball, J. W., Kinney, E. M., & Taylor, B. A. (2006). Activity schedules, computer technology, and teaching children with autism spectrum disorders. *Focus on Autism and Other Developmental Disabilities*, 21, 14-24.

Thiemann, K. S., & Goldstein, H. (2001). Social stories, written text cues, and video feedback: Effects on social communication of children with autism. *Journal of Applied Behavior Analysis*, 34, 425-446.

Weatherby, A. M., Schuler, A. L., & Prizant, B. M. (1997) Enhancing language and communication development: Theoretical foundations. In D. J. Cohen & F. R. Volkmar (Eds.), *Handbook of autism and pervasive developmental disorders* (2nd ed., pp. 513-538). New York: Wiley.

Wright, L.A. (2007). *Utilizing social stories to reduce problem behavior and increase pro-social behavior in young children with autism.* Unpublished doctoral dissertation, University of Missouri, Columbia.

RECOMMENDED RESOURCES

This is by no means a complete list; but rather a few choice resources recommended by the author.

TEACCH

Treatment and Education of Autistic and Communication Handicapped Children/Adults
www.teacch.com
Founded by the late Dr. Eric Schopler, and directed by Dr. Gary Mesibov, the University of North Carolina at Chapel Hill's School of Medicine has been the home of the TEACCH Program since the early 1970s. The TEACCH approach includes a focus on the person with ASD and the development of an individualized program around his or her skills, strengths, interests, and needs. The major priorities include centering on the individual, understanding the autism spectrum, adopting appropriate adaptations, and a broadly-based intervention strategy building on skills and interests. By focusing on the individual, we mean that the *person is the priority*, rather than any philosophical notion such as inclusion, discrete trial training, facilitated communication, etc. TEACCH emphasizes *individualized assessment* to understand the individual and to acknowledge and better understand "the culture of autism," suggesting that people with ASD are part of a distinct group with common characteristics that are different, not inferior, to others. TEACCH provides extensive introductory and advanced training nationally and internationally, to parents, teachers, psychologists, therapists, physicians, and other professionals.

The Gray Center for Social Learning and Understanding

www.thegraycenter.org
The Gray Center is an organization dedicated to individuals with autism spectrum disorders and those who work alongside them to improve mutual understanding. The social impairment in ASD is approached as a shared impairment, with shared responsibility. Social understanding strategies such as Social Stories™ and Comic Strip Conversations were developed to improve social understanding on both sides of the social equation. The clear, literal, and reassuring writing style of Catherine Faherty's books is characteristic of Social Stories™.

OASIS@MAAP

www.aspergersyndrome.org
The Online Asperger Syndrome Information and Support (OASIS) center has joined with MAAP Services for Autism and Asperger Syndrome to create a single resource for families, individuals, and medical professionals who deal with the challenges of Asperger's Syndrome, autism, and Pervasive Developmental Disorder Not Otherwise Specified (PDD/NOS). This website provides articles, educational resources, links to local, national and international support groups, sources of professional help, lists of camps and schools, conference information, recommended reading, and moderated support message boards. The website resources are an addition to the annual conference, newsletter email and phone support provided by MAAP Services.

ANI (Autism Network International)

www.autreat.com

Autism Network International is an autistic-run self-help and advocacy organization for autistic people. The philosophy and goals of ANI, stated on their website, are that the best advocates for autistic people are autistic people themselves (ANI is run by and for autistic people); autistic lives are meaningful and worthwhile lives; supports for autistic people should be aimed at helping them to compensate, navigate and function in the world, not at changing them into non-autistic people or isolating them from the world (ANI provides a forum for autistic people to share information, peer support, and tips for coping and problem-solving); autistic people of all ages and all levels of ability and skill are entitled to adequate and appropriate support services; autistic people have characteristically autistic styles of relating to others, which should be respected and appreciated rather than modified to make them "fit in" (ANI provides a social outlet for autistic people to explore and participate in autistic social experiences). ANI sponsors an annual retreat-style conference (Autreat) run by autistic people, for autistic people and their friends. Autreat is three days of continuous immersion in an autism-friendly environment.

GRASP (Global and Regional Asperger Syndrome Partnership)

www.grasp.org

GRASP is an educational and advocacy organization serving individuals on the autism spectrum. GRASP runs a support group network, educational outreach, and is an informational clearinghouse on issues relating to the autism spectrum. GRASP's bylaws stipulate that the Executive Director, 100% of the Advisory Board, and 50% of the Board of Directors of GRASP must be diagnosed with either autism, Asperger's Syndrome, or a pervasive developmental disorder.

ABOUT THE AUTHOR

Photo by Marilyn Ferikes

At age thirteen, when volunteering at a summer day camp for children with special needs in suburban Chicago, Catherine knew immediately that this would be her life's work. Her early education and training in the mid-1970s was at Eastern Michigan University in Ypsilanti, Michigan, where she worked each afternoon after her classes at the lab school for exceptional children on campus. Since 1985 she has been affiliated with the TEACCH Program, first as a classroom teacher and later as a psychoeducational specialist at the Asheville TEACCH Center, one of North Carolina's nine regional TEACCH Centers through the University of North Carolina at Chapel Hill. Weekly diagnostic evaluations for children and adults; educational sessions for parents, children, and adults with ASD; social groups for adults with autism; educational and support groups for parents; and consulting to school systems fill her days at the TEACCH Center. Catherine is a Lead Teacher and Trainer for TEACCH trainings nationally and internationally; she helps to create and develop new training models; and she wrote the manual, *TEACCH Structured Teaching Assessment: Guides to Individualizing the Schedule and Work System*. Her book *Asperger's …What Does It Mean To Me?* (Future Horizons, 2000) was the first of its kind written for children and youth with ASD. Translated into several languages, this reader-friendly book helps build self-awareness and self-esteem for verbal children with ASD, along with providing a wealth of Structured Teaching strategies for their parents and teachers. Her book *Understanding Death and Illness and What They Teach About Life* (Future Horizons, 2008) was awarded the 2009 Autism Society of America Outstanding Book Award in the Family/Social Division.

As a member of Team Social Stories™, Catherine Faherty is one of the few world-wide authorized trainers of Social Stories™, promoting and teaching Social Stories™ as introduced and taught by Carol Gray and The Gray Center for Social Learning and Understanding.

I hope that this book will nurture understanding within families, classrooms, worksites, and communities for people with ASD and their communication partners.

I am especially grateful for the encouragement I received during the writing of this book from Steven Love, Director of the Asheville TEACCH Center who keeps supporting my writing projects; Vaya Papageorgiou, my friend and colleague in Greece who first urged me to write this book; Janna Zonder for proofreading and consultation; Ginger Graziano, for technical support; Kelly Gilpin, my editor at Future Horizons who is the most gracious person I know; my family and friends who checked in with me during the writing of this book; Ismene Collins, my mom, who gave me a foundation of creativity in teaching; Nicholas and Kai Faherty, my son and grandson, who give me love, laughter, and good food; and of course John Faherty, whose constant selfless support is truly awesome.

Catherine Faherty, May 2010

INDEX

A

Y

Z

Extend teaching and learning with these great resources!

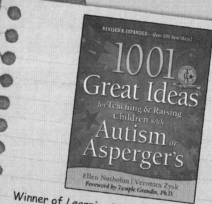